John Hilton

Trust and Love

For Philip
Who helped me find
my way to Christ.

xxx

©2015 John Hilton
All rights reserved. This book may not be reproduced in any form, in whole or in part, without written permission from the author.

Also by John Hilton
Seven Contrasting Histories
Cracked
Tales of People
Spinning and Telling
Dear Love
All This Expression
Alphabet of 26 Parts
Shadowy Tales
Hotchpotch
Words
Watching the Sky
Collected Poems
Tales*
Waiting for the Earth to Turn to Green
Poems 1993-2015*

All available on Kindle.
* = Also available in paperback

A forward by Philip John Fowles

I was delighted when John Hilton kindly asked me to pen this forward to his anthology of prayers and I commend this book to you as a thought provoking addition to your Christian prayer life.

John is a committed Christian whom I have come to know through his work as a volunteer visitor in our award winning homes for elderly residents at St Monica Trust in Bristol where his boundless energy and fun we have come to appreciate and enjoy.

Within the following pages you will undoubtedly find words of comfort and solace, yet also thoughts that challenge perceptions in the prayers that John has so beautifully crafted from his lifetime experiences.

I trust you enjoy and use this anthology with as much pleasure as I had in writing this forward.

Philip John Fowles,
URC Preacher & Pastoral Coordinator,
St Monica Trust

author's note

Many of the poems in this volume have appeared in previous volumes of my poetry. Most of them have been revised, sometimes only very slightly, other times rather more, for this volume.

Despite this, it is not, in the traditional sense, a selected poems, rather a collection of poems centred around questions and issues of faith. It is not a guide book to religion, merely a book of poems I have written as part of my own quest to answer those questions of identity and purpose that have occurred to me, as they have to countless others, as I grow older and my life takes on greater fullness.

The date below each poem refers to the completion date. Those poems that were lightly revised have the original completion dates. Some of the newer works were drafted several years before this and left aside before being knocked into shape during November 2015, which turned out to be a very productive month for my poetry. One week in November also saw several new poems drafted and completed.

Thank you, Philip for your support, encouragement and writing the preface for me.

Thanks to Jenny, for everything. Without you, my wife and best friend, none of this would have happened.

This is me and these are my prayers.

Thank you,
John Hilton, April, 2016.

Contents

A forward by Philip John Fowles.......................3
author's note...5
Love is All Around [take one]..........................8
Love Imperfect...10
Love Over Rules...12
The Merest Touch of Grace............................14
Life in Christ...17
All Hell Must End...19
A Child's Last Prayer....................................21
Waiting Still..23
My Half-Brother..25
Shopping Centre Chapel................................29
Questions of Faith..31
Searching for a Return..................................34
Words for God...42
Eden's Blood...45
Journey..47
Finding God..51
Planks..53
Among the Damned......................................54
Of Credence and Innocence...........................56
What is Love?...59
Love is All Around [take two].........................64

Love is All Around [take one]

'Love is all around'
can be read as

the title of a
charming pop song
from the sixties

or a boast from
the free lovers of
the same decade.

But for those who
attempt to follow in
the spiritual footsteps
of our Lord Jesus Christ

it is no more or less
than a statement of fact.

God is Love and
God is everywhere

and therefore
Love truly is
all around

9

**every single
one of us.**

23rd November 2015

Love Imperfect

Memories of hurt and
remembrance of failure
seem all useless junk.

So can we not
just let it go?

Endless cupboards
filled with regrets.

Such needless and
heavy burdens that
we never seem to
be able to find
the time nor
the method
to wash out
of our minds.

And yet
every loss and
every failure
helped mould us
into the people

we are today.

**For we are all
the sum of each
and every one of
our experiences
and to learn to
love our failures
as dearly as
our successes
is to know
and to love
ourselves.**

18th November, 2015

Love Over Rules

Whenever faith is replaced
by a set of rules and a
focus on mere appearances

and whenever the god of love
is shunted aside by
mortal fears and
dread of eternity

and whenever the bliss
of true and heavenly peace
is trampled under foot by
the dogs of holy war

and whenever rich men
sit in the front rows
of the churches we built
in the names of our God

then the promise of
the coming of Heaven
to this Earth that
suffers under all this
hate and envy and

jealousy and conceit

**will be delayed
yet longer until
the day comes
when each and
every one of us
learns to feel
to the full
and act upon
in our every
thought and deed
the true beauty
of pure and
universal
Love.**

**God is Love
and
Love is Good.**

18th November 2015

The Merest Touch of Grace

Sitting in this wooden pew
the pale stone arches
upwards and in so doing
gives my soul the space
to rest from the everyday
crowding and crowing
of the city of my dreams.

I feel the love of God
caress me and
gently illuminate

the calmness within
the very core
of my being.

This tiny spark
of God's Grace
animates my soul

and gives me a purpose
that is far greater
than my mortal flesh,
and strangely I feel

in this so public space
a touch of God's presence
that is, in a quietly
profound fashion,
more intimate than
any I have felt before.

And so though I remain
a lost and tainted soul,

at last I can now see
that, although I have
no idea where the key
to this peace lies
or if upon finding it
I will discover the Grace
that will fit key to lock,

from this moment onward
I am sure the sanctuary
I am seeking
is here already.

Indeed
it has been here
all the while
waiting

**for me
to feel it.**

26th September 2008

Life in Christ

Why do you choose
to waste your precious
time and limited
energies devoting
yourself to endlessly
praying to Jesus
in the hope of boosting
your chances of
Heaven's blessings
when you could
be less selfish and
devote your life
to helping others
carry their burdens
and heal their scars
and shed their sins?

For then,
and only then,
will you be able
to truly claim
to be doing
the holy work
that our Lord

**Jesus Christ
set for us.**

**God is Love
and to Love
is to be holy.**

24th November 2015

All Hell Must End

Truly I tell you
there can be
no soul in Heaven
while any Hell
still exists.

For nobody who
truly follows
the words of
our Lord Jesus
could ever
seriously consider
entering the
Kingdom
of Heaven
while even
one lost soul
remained
in Hell.

Such was
the covenant.

Such is

**the truth of
unconditional
Love.**

**Anything less
is simply
missing
the point.**

18th November 2015

A Child's Last Prayer

Dear God,
I'm sorry I've been a bad girl
I don't mean to be,
but sometimes I forget.

Please don't hurt me any more.

Is Mr Buchan really an angel?
He says he is.
He says he is helping me
to be a good girl
by punishing me when I'm bad.
But he hurts me
and makes me cry,
and if I tell my daddy
he'll make my daddy die.

So will you please tell daddy
so he can make it stop?

I really will try
to be good
but I don't know
if I can do it.

Please, please Mr God,
don't hurt me any more.
I hurt so much already.

Father David says
you love everybody.
But that means
you love Mr Buchan.
And I hurt so much already.

Please God,
just one last wish
I know it's not my time yet,
but will you forgive me
if I join you now?

20th September, 2006.

Waiting Still

I sat
and I waited
but you
did not come.

The evening faded
into the night and
I slept in my chair
until the sun emerged
and shone on a figure with
head resting on the table.

Through so many
long days
and such
lonely weeks
and endless years.

In other rooms
with other desks.

And yet,
though so much
has changed,

still I am here

**and still
I am waiting
for you.**

7ᵗʰ February, 2008

My Half-Brother

He may have been
God's only son
but I was one of
four brothers
and my mother
birthed us five.
Four siblings and
our half-brother.

My name is James
and I was her second born,
eldest bar Him,
and in any case,
as I have said, He
was only a half-brother
though my father treated
and loved him like a son.

And let there be no doubt
that he was truly God
or possibly just one aspect
I cannot be sure.
I claim no deep understanding
of such things.

He was obviously divine
though it took his undying
and returning to my sight
to give me the confidence
to say so, though, if you
look deep enough into
the right places, you will
see I fasted from the time
of the last supper until
I saw my half-brother
arisen from the grave.

And later I took my place
on the Apostolic Council,
a leader who tried so hard
to bridge the gap
between the new Christians
and the Jews.

And I got so close.

But now,
with Festus dead,
Ananus has grown bold
and I sit here and await
my death that

will flow from his words.

I care not
for I have played my part
as best I could.

The Heavenly father
knows my heart,
understands why
I doubted
and why I then
understood.

Soon I shall pass-over
from this mortal coil
to the Heavenly realms
and join my departed
friends and family.

And most of all
I shall speak with
my half-brother again.
Hear his words
and feel his grace.
So now the time has come
to bid you well
and take my leave.

**My name is James
and I am a son
of the Mother of God.**

13th March 2009

Shopping Centre Chapel

Hush.

**Slip discretely from the
crowded street of shops
and into the quiet chapel.**

**Gregorian chant plays low,
just this side of audible,
deepening the feeling of
space with this room set aside
for contemplation and
meditation as
the sound enriches the silence
rather than distracting from it.**

**Take the time
to listen carefully
to the quietest sound
many people never
think to hear.**

**And, thus,
listen to
the whispered harmonies**

**and subtly complex
rhythms that flow through
the very essence that
is our soul.**

8th October 2015

Questions of Faith

Your long slim fingers
gently caress
the burgundy glass
and accompanying
bottle that sits
nearly spent
in front of you.

Your eyes drift around
its fragile form
but nothing registers.

So you close your eyes
and bow your head
in a gesture of penitence
as hollow as your words of regret

The you look into my face
with a pain so vast
a world swarms within it.

You ask me
'Why?
Why should I believe

in a God who
left me like this?'

And I told you of a God
who knew only love.

Who was the essence
of love itself.

And I spoke of a forgiveness
that comes both from God
and from ourselves.

I tried to show you
how strength can
come after and from pain,
allowing you to overcome
all your weakness
and sense of loss.

And I spoke
of humanity
and humility.

And of the love
we held within ourselves
and finally of the love

we keep out,
too frightened
to accept its challenge
or its promise.

And I paused.

For though I believed
in every word I had said,
I was no longer sure
any of it was true.

29th July, 2007

Searching for a Return

Can you hear me?

-

As no doubt you know already
I came here to look for you
but I could not see you, just
as I could not see you
where I was before
or in any other place
I have access to.

-

But still I am looking
for looking is what I do.
It defines all I am now,
or at least marks all that
still matters.

-

For now you have gone
from me and mine.

-

Don't get me wrong.
Of course I know
all too well
where you are,
it is just that
I cannot see you for the
simple reason that I remain
unready to receive that
singular vision.

-

But I can wait long
for have I not already
yearned for so much
long time already?

Patience, so they say, is
one of the seven Heavenly
virtues and may well be the
only virtue that remains
available as an option for
my sad, fallen soul.

**But oh it has already
been so long a wait
and I am very tired,
have been so very
tired for so much
slow time as a
succession of days
that has long passed
beyond all counting
have come and gone
to mark my solitude.**

-

**I am now a truly humble
being and yet it would
seem that humility is
no longer enough and
something more,
something different,
is clearly required but
just what it is I cannot
see or understand and
maybe it is in that fact
the answer to my
problem lies.**

I just don't know but
still I cling to the few
slender straws that
are still mine to claim.

-

There is almost nowhere
in this world that I cannot
go and yet it is not enough,
for my true home is not
here nor anywhere that I
can reach and I am so
alone and can remember
the true, pure love that once
surrounded me and the light
and the wisdom and lastly
the power that led to the
pride that in turn was to
cost me all that really
mattered, leaving me here
wandering the world
without you.

-

I can see the smallest leaf on

the most distant of mountains
but I cannot see you.

I can follow every wave
on every sea, but you
are beyond my vision.

I can hear every whisper
and cry of every one of
your creatures but I
cannot hear you.

And my grief fills all
that was once my soul.
So I cry in the darkness,
sigh in the wilderness
and grieve in the silence.

-

Can you hear me?

Or is your silence proof
there is no return
for your fallen son?

Many a time I have seen

little flickers, shadows of
your grace and mercy but
never have I been allowed
even the slightest sign of
of you or the faintest whisper
of your voice.

And so I shall remain here
to wander for eternity
across this world which
it was never my place to
try to save or protect.

I have heard many who
are so sure that they know
my purpose and my role
but although I do not know
or understand either of
those things, I do know
they are all wrong and
they are as clueless
as I am as to your plan
and their and my roles
within it.

-

But still I am tired
knowing that there is
no rest for me.

I am barren,
without kin,
and so
completely
alone.

I have only myself
for both company
and blame.

And so I walk on.

Seeing.

Hearing.

Touching.

Everything,
except you.

I am alone.

I am forgotten.

I am sorry.

I am waiting.

I am still here.

Can you hear me?

13th March, 2009

Words for God

Omniscient.

**Just for once,
really think about it.**

Omniscient.

**Easy to say but have you ever
stopped to wonder
exactly what
that word really means?**

**It means
He knows
everything
and He remembers
*all of it.***

**Every thing you have ever done
and, more importantly,
exactly why you did it.**

**Every thought you've ever had
and every evasion, every lie and**

every half-truth you have ever told
yourself.

Nothing is overlooked
or forgotten.

As He is also omnipresent
you can be assured
he misses nothing,
no matter how small,
or however well
you deceive yourself.

Every right thing you did
for the wrong reasons and also
every wrong act
you carried out with pure intent.

Every time your chest inflated with Pride,
every put-down and every false modesty.

If you think God will judge you
by your actions
then I have to tell you
you are mistaken,
because only God
truly knows your motives.

And there can be no escape
for He is omnipotent,
in other words,
all powerful and
powerful in all places.

And if you still feel sure and safe
then you clearly
have not been listening.

16th December 2009

Eden's Blood

Sitting in your chair
quietly reading
and thinking
you suddenly realise
the rest of the world
has receded from you.

It's still out there
but it's another's world,
yours no longer.

And so you spiral inwards
finally coming to rest
in the one place
you swore you'd never visit
ever again.

But here you are,
back once more.

In with the grey
the black
and the blood,
standing before

the black book of your sins.

You are your own judge
to a jury of your past.

How do you plead this time?

There is the sword
there your mitre,
and somewhere
behind it all
is you.

Once more I ask,

how do you plead?

10th December, 2007

Journey

Move
ever onward.

To stop
is to end
and to end
is to die.

So keep on
moving,
climbing
to the peaks
of ambition
and plodding
grimly through
the lows
as you kick
your slow way
through the
undergrowth.

Keep on
striving.

Onwards to
a destination
that may simply
turn out
to have never
existed outside
of your dreams

and the empty
promises from
well meaning
fools and the
professional
parasites who
worship Mammon

but think themselves
to be their
own masters.

You must
keep on
pushing.

Keep on
moving
forward.

**Minute after minute
after hour after hour
after day after week
after month after
year after decade**

until

**finally you find
you can go forward
no longer and
so your journey
comes to its end**

**and your life
switches off.**

**And as you vacate
your body**

**so your soul
vanishes from
the sight of
all who are
still only part
of their way**

**through their
own journey.**

23rd November 2015

Finding God

Where is God?

**God is nowhere
to be seen**

**and yet
He is everywhere.**

**He is where you live
and where you work.**

**He is with your friends and
he is where your enemies
gather and your rivals plot.**

**As I have said
He is nowhere
to be seen
but**

**if He is
in your heart**

then

**He can be felt
everywhere
and in
everything.**

18th November, 2015

Planks

Because
we live our lives
above the abyss,
the dark void
of despair,
it is best to hope
for more than planks
under our feet
and for friends
to hold us
should we start to fall.

12th March, 2007

Among the Damned

You don't realise it yet
but he walks among you,
merging into the background
as if he had always been there.

Perhaps he was?

Count the signs.

The metal leg
that will not bend.
The glass eye
that yet sees all.
The way he never
speaks the number six.

Heed the signs.

He knows your name.
He knows your life.

He is your fears.
He owns your dreams.

And he is only here
because you invited him in.

You accepted the deal
without understanding
the terms of the trade.

But now there is
no place for refunds
or possibility of exchange.

You took the money
now he is here to collect.

So go with your master.

Tempus Fugit.

But you have
nowhere left
to run.

4th December, 2007

Of Credence and Innocence

When I was a child
you told me
the world I had recently joined
was a fair one.

Justice was implicit
in the very air that I breathed.

The righteous prosper
and the damned go to Hell
and all things will come
to those who pray and wait.

Further more you explained
how the God of Love
was a vengeful God,

that questions imply a doubt
that saddens your God,

a God that can only be reached
on the celestial phone
in your church.

How your title
should be taken literally,
that only you may touch
me there,

and how kisses can be holy
if given by a holy man

and how God gave us animals
to possess and to eat
and eternity can be heard
in the heartbeat of God,

and women are only here
to tempt us from
the pure path your God
has laid before us
and wealth is only here
so Satan can enslave us,
that a secret kept
with a holy man
is a sacred thing indeed.

But now that I am old
and my youth long since died,
I can say
in a voice so cold

**with despair
that almost
nothing you said
was true.**

Circa 2005

What is Love?

I've been thinking
about love.

Love can mean
everything
or
it can mean
nothing at all.

You can neither
see or locate it
as it is not
an object
but rather
a state of mind,
an attitude,
and a perception.

But what is it?

When we hear
a friend or colleague
is 'in love' we
nod sagely as if

we knew exactly
what was happening.

But let us give
a little thought
to what that word
really means.

What is Love?

Is it lust and desire?

Is it empathy?

Is it a need?

Is it a cherishing?

Is it a longing?

Is it a desire to possess?

Is it all of those things?

Or is it none of them?

Are Love and lust

two sides of
the same thing?

Or are they
mutually
opposed?

Or it could be
they have nothing
to do with
each other.

Is love
something you *do*
or something you *feel?*
Or is it something
that happens *to* you?

Can love ever be
destructive?

Or when it seems to,
is it taking the blame
due to lust, envy and
possessiveness?

Perhaps it is time we

found separate words
for all the different
definitions of love?

Have we reached
the stage where,
by meaning everything,
'love' has finally come
to mean nothing at all?

Perhaps, as a poet, I
am expected to be wise
and be able to tell all
who read this words
the answers to all these
questions?

But I'm not
and I don't
have a clue.

Disappointed?

You shouldn't be.

All I will say,
in ending this

meandering poem,
is that Caritas
gets my vote
every time
though
faith and hope
run it close.

Go figure it out
for yourself.

27th November, 2015

Love is All Around [take two]

What is it
I feel when
I believe
I truly feel
the presence
of God?

It is warmth
and yet it
is can not
be called
heat.

It helps me
to feel safe
and yet it is
not wall or lock.

With its presence
I feel surer of
my path through
life's twists and
pitfalls and yet
it is neither map

nor book of rules.

I could
call it love,
but love
means so many
different things
in so many
confusing ways
to so many
different people
it can no longer
serve as a term
of description.

Should I call it God?

But God has
a thousand
and more
different names
all invented by
mere mortals and all,
in truth, no more
than labels
for something
far beyond our abilities

to fully see let alone
attempt to understand.

Perhaps,
instead of all this
internal debate
and reduction
I should just
accept its presence
and let others find
their own ways
to this place
within ourselves
wherein lies
a true peace and
a true love.

23rd November, 2015

Made in the USA
Charleston, SC
26 April 2016